Get set... GO!

Summer

Ruth Thomson

Contents

W

FRANKLIN WATTS

LONDON • NEW YORK • SYDNEY

# It's summer!

Summer is warm and sunny.
Flowers bloom and scent the air.
Bees buzz from flower to flower,
gathering nectar and pollen.

Butterflies flutter about.
Grasshoppers and crickets sing
all day long, hidden in long grass.
Dragonflies dart over ponds
hunting gnats and other insects.

Wheat, oats and barley ripen
in the sunshine.
Farmers reap them with combine harvesters.

Families go on holiday to the seaside.
The children dig in the sand.
They collect stones and shells.

Drying flowers

Get ready

✔ Flowers with long stems
✔ String

...Get set

Pick some flowers on a sunny day.
Choose ones not quite in bloom.

⇒❀⇒❀⇒❀ *Go!*

Tie several stems together with string.
Tie them tightly, because they will shrink.
Hang them upside down
in a dark, dry place.
After several weeks,
they will be papery dry.

Dried flower pictures

Get ready

✔ Dried flowers   ✔ Pencils

✔ Stiff card   ✔ Glue

...Get set

Draw an outline of your picture
on the card.

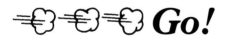 Go!

Stick the dried flowers on to the card,
following your outline.

Lavender bags

Get ready

✔ Dried lavender ✔ Fabric ✔ Pinking scissors
✔ Pins ✔ Ribbon ✔ Needle and thread

...Get set

Dry some lavender. Break off the flowers.

⇒ ⇒ ⇒ *Go!*

Cut two small squares of fabric.
Pin the right sides together.
Sew along three sides.
Turn the bag right side out.
Fill it with lavender.
Sew running stitches around the top.
Pull the ends of the thread tight.
Make a knot. Tie ribbon around the bag.

Leaf rubbings

Get ready

✔ Paper
✔ Wax crayons or a soft pencil
✔ Different sorts of leaves

...Get set

Pick leaves of all shapes and sizes.

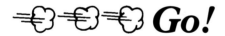 **Go!**

Put a piece of paper on top of
one of the leaves.
Feel where the edges are.
Rub over it with the wax crayon.
Watch a pattern appear.
Make a whole sheet of leaf rubbings
to use as wrapping paper.

 # Painted pebbles

Get ready

✔ Pebbles of all shapes and sizes

✔ Nailbrush

✔ Paintbrush

✔ Thick paint

✔ Newspaper

✔ Clear varnish

...Get set

Scrub and rinse the pebbles.
Leave them to dry.

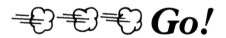 **Go!**

Look at the pebbles from all sides.
What does each one remind you of?
Paint the pebbles.
Leave them to dry.
Coat the pebbles with varnish
if you want them to look shiny.

Shell pictures

Get ready

✔ Shells
✔ Thick card
✔ Strong glue

...Get set

Wash your shells in warm water.
Leave them to dry.
Sort them by size, shape and colour.

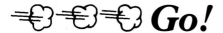 **Go!**

Glue the shells on to card
to make all sorts of pictures.

Sand pictures

Get ready

✔ Shells or
     other objects

✔ Stiff card

✔ Sand

✔ Glue

✔ Pencil

...Get set

Put some shells or other objects
on the card.

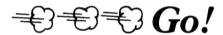 **Go!**

Spread glue around the objects
and over the rest of the card.
Sprinkle sand on top of the glue.
Leave the glue to dry.
Take off the objects.
Shake any loose sand off the card.

Grow a sunflower

Get ready

- ✔ Sunflower seeds
- ✔ Trowel
- ✔ Watering can
- ✔ Plant markers
- ✔ Pen
- ✔ Bamboo cane

...Get set

Sow some seeds in May
in a sunny spot near a wall.
Make sure you plant them
at least one big stride apart.

⟨⟩⟨⟩⟨⟩ *Go!*

Water the plants regularly.
When they are as tall as you are,
tie them to a tall cane.
They will flower from July to September.

Lemonade

Get ready

- ✔ 2 lemons
- ✔ 30 grams white or brown sugar
- ✔ 6 cups water
- ✔ Plastic or china jug
- ✔ Knife
- ✔ Lemon squeezer

...Get set

Wash the lemons and peel them thinly.
Put the peel and sugar into the jug.
Ask an adult to help you boil
the water and pour it into the jug.
Leave the mixture to cool.

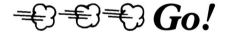 **Go!**

Squeeze the juice out of the lemons.
Add it to the jug and stir.
Serve the lemonade with ice.

Insect brooches

Get ready

- ✔ Tracing paper
- ✔ Pencil
- ✔ Stiff card
- ✔ Glue
- ✔ Scissors
- ✔ Brooch pin
- ✔ Lace
- ✔ Glitter
- ✔ Sequins

...Get set

Fold the tracing paper in half.
Draw one half of an insect
along the folded edge.
Cut through both layers.

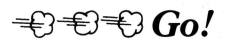 **Go!**

Open out the insect shape.
Draw round it on to card. Cut it out.
Glue on a brooch pin.
Decorate the insect prettily.

Index

Photographic Credits:
Heather Angel 11, 19;
Paul Bricknell 17, 21; Chris
Fairclough Colour Library 3;
Peter Millard 5, 6-7, 9, 13,
15, 23.

©1993 Franklin Watts

Paperback edition 1997

Franklin Watts
96 Leonard Street
London EC2A 4RH

Franklin Watts Australia
14 Mars Road
Lane Cove
NSW 2066

UK ISBN 0 7496 1301 7
              (hardback)
              0 7496 2646 1
              (paperback)

Editor: Pippa Pollard
Design: Ruth Levy
Cover design: Mike Davis
Artwork: Ruth Levy

A CIP catalogue record for
this book is available from the
British Library

Dewey Decimal Classification
745.5

Printed in Malaysia

24